J. PIERPONT MORGAN

MORGAN

INDUSTRIALIST AND FINANCIER

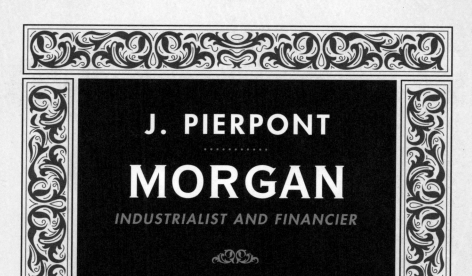

J. PIERPONT

MORGAN

INDUSTRIALIST AND FINANCIER

by Michael Burgan

Content Adviser: Gregory DL Morris,
Principal of Enterprise & Industry
Historic Research, New York City

Reading Adviser: Rosemary G. Palmer, Ph.D.,
Department of Literacy, College of Education,
Boise State University

COMPASS POINT BOOKS ✦ MINNEAPOLIS, MINNESOTA

Compass Point Books
3109 West 50th Street, #115
Minneapolis, MN 55410

Visit Compass Point Books on the Internet at *www.compasspointbooks.com*
or e-mail your request to *custserv@compasspointbooks.com*

Editor: Sue Vander Hook
Page Production: Noumenon Creative
Photo Researcher: Svetlana Zhurkin
Cartographer: XNR Productions, Inc.
Library Consultant: Kathleen Baxter

Art Director: Jaime Martens
Creative Director: Keith Griffin
Editorial Director: Carol Jones
Managing Editor: Catherine Neitge

Library of Congress Cataloging-in-Publication Data
Burgan, Michael
  J. Pierpont Morgan: Industrialist and Financier / by Michael Burgan.
    p. cm.—(Signature lives)
  Includes bibliographical references and index.
  ISBN-13: 978-0-7565-1890-5 (hardcover)
  ISBN-10: 0-7565-1890-3 (hardcover)
  ISBN-13: 978-0-7565-1987-2 (paperback)
  ISBN-10: 0-7565-1987-X (paperback)
  1. Morgan, J. Pierpont. (John Pierpont), 1837–1931—Juvenile literature.
2. Bankers—United States—Biography—Juvenile literature. 3. Capitalists
and financiers—United States—Biography—Juvenile literature. 1. Title.
II. Series.
  HG2463.M6B87 2007
  332.1092—dc22   2006002996

MODERN AMERICA

Starting in the late 19th century, advancements in all areas of human activity transformed an old world into a new and modern place. Inventions prompted rapid shifts in lifestyle, and scientific discoveries began to alter the way humanity viewed itself. Beginning with World War I, warfare took place on a global scale, and ideas such as nationalism and communism showed that countries were taking a larger view of their place in the world. The combination of all these changes continues to produce what we know as the modern world.

Table of Contents

1

THE DEAL
OF A LIFETIME

Chapter

⤜⋙×⋘⤛

J. Pierpont Morgan sat in his plush, wood-paneled library in his New York City home on Madison Avenue. He was a hefty man, and his large purplish-red nose protruded noticeably over his bushy mustache. Between his lips he typically clenched a Cuban cigar so large that it was called Hercules' Club. Morgan was one of the wealthiest, most powerful businessmen in the United States. Wherever he went, he commanded respect and wielded control. One person said that a visit from Morgan made him feel "as if a gale had blown through the house."

Morgan carefully studied the man across the table from him. Charles Schwab, president of Carnegie Steel Company in Pittsburgh, Pennsylvania, was there to discuss a business deal with Morgan.

For more than 40 years, Morgan had been establishing, acquiring, and merging businesses. He was so successful that by 1900, he had more money than the annual budget of the United States. He controlled railroads, banks, and a large steel mill. One newspaper reporter said Morgan had "greater force, greater character, and greater intellect ... than any other man on Wall Street." Those traits won him the trust of investors, politicians, and business owners.

Schwab wanted Morgan to buy Carnegie Steel, which included eight steel mills. Its founder and owner, Andrew Carnegie, had made it the biggest, richest steel company in America. Steel was in high demand, especially since the rapidly growing railroad industry was using it more and more in place of iron to build railroad cars, tracks, buildings, and bridges. Iron had to be replaced every few months. Steel, on the other hand, lasted for years. The steelmaking process involved heating iron until it was molten, or liquid, and burning out elements like carbon. What was left was a much

Charles M. Schwab (1862–1939)

Iron was converted to steel at Carnegie Steel Company in Pittsburgh, Pennsylvania, in the late 1800s.

stronger material that could be formed into shapes.

Morgan questioned Schwab for hours at the January 1901 meeting. Was he serious about selling Carnegie Steel? Would Schwab help him create a company that would be the giant of the steel industry? What was Carnegie's price? Schwab said he would ask Carnegie how much he wanted. Morgan replied, "Well, if you can get a price from Carnegie, I don't know but what I'll undertake [agree to] it."

For the next few weeks, Schwab discussed the deal with Carnegie. Finally, Carnegie wrote down a number—$480 million (about $10.3 billion today). Schwab rushed to Morgan, who looked at the amount, looked at Schwab, and said, "I accept this price."

On February 25, 1901, J. Pierpont Morgan announced his purchase of Carnegie Steel and the creation of U.S. Steel Corporation. He combined Carnegie Steel and his own company, Federal Steel Company, into one huge corporation. Morgan now owned a company worth a billion dollars, the largest and richest in the world. It produced two-thirds of America's steel. The company owned 115 ships, several railroad lines, and vast areas of land where iron and coal were mined. Many investors put money into the company because they believed it would do well. In return, they would receive some of the profits.

Andrew Carnegie (1835–1919)

Morgan had made the biggest deal of his lifetime. He would make other smart business decisions that would help him retain his position as one of the wealthiest people in the world. He would also pave the way for the United States to become a world leader in industry. His status as a prominent, powerful banker would bring his country out of a financial crisis more than once. Morgan believed his business efforts made the United States a stronger nation.

Some would criticize Morgan and call him a plutocrat, someone whose power is based on wealth. In 1910, a U.S. senator called him "a beefy, red-faced, thick-necked financial bully, drunk with wealth and power." Yet Morgan helped strengthen the country in its post-Civil War struggles. He was also a great philanthropist who gave money to hospitals, churches, universities, botanical gardens, and museums. His gifts of art and ancient artifacts to the American Museum of Natural History filled an entire wing. His private library at his Fifth Avenue home eventually became the Morgan Library, where his vast collection of rare art, books, and personal papers is on public display.

Andrew Carnegie (1835–1919) is a classic example of a rags-to-riches story. A Scottish immigrant, he arrived in the United States in 1848 with little money. Settling in Pittsburgh, Pennsylvania, he worked at low-paying jobs before becoming a telegraph operator for the Pennsylvania Railroad. He made $35 per month. Carnegie saved his money, took out loans, and invested in several companies. By the 1870s, he owned a steel company and was known as the Steel King. Carnegie used some of his vast wealth to start public libraries, build Carnegie Hall in New York City, and start organizations to promote world peace.

2 CHILD OF WEALTH

Chapter

ele❧ele

On April 17, 1837, John Pierpont Morgan was born in Hartford, Connecticut. His father, Junius Spencer Morgan, was a successful partner in a local business. His mother, Juliet Pierpont Morgan, was the daughter of a Boston, Massachusetts, minister.

Junius and Juliet nicknamed their son Bub but later called him Pierpont. As a baby, he was often ill. Although he recovered from his early illnesses, he remained a sickly child. His health kept him from starting school until he was about 7 years old, but by then he had learned many things at home from his parents. By the time Pierpont was 9 years old, the family had grown to four children: Pierpont, Sarah, Mary, and Junius Jr.

Because his family was wealthy, Pierpont had

An 1847 photograph of John Pierpont Morgan and his sisters, Sarah (left) and Mary

Juliet Pierpont Morgan (1816–1884)

adventures few children his age experienced. Railroad travel was new and expensive. But when Pierpont was just 3 years old, his parents took him by train from Hartford to New Haven, Connecticut. At age 7, he rode the first train to travel between

Hartford and Boston.

Sometimes Pierpont traveled alone by train to Boston, where he visited his grandparents, the Reverend John Pierpont and his wife Mary. Pierpont especially enjoyed his time with his grandfather, who exposed him to many ideas, including his view of slavery. His grandfather and some people in his church strongly opposed slavery when many Americans accepted it. Pierpont and his family were members of the Episcopal Church, whose members usually didn't challenge slavery.

When Pierpont was 10 years old, his other grandfather, Joseph Morgan, died and left his son Junius an estate worth $1 million (about $22 million today). The Morgans were now one of the richest families in Connecticut. Junius had learned a lot about business from his father, and now he passed his knowledge on to Pierpont. When Pierpont wasn't in school, his father took him to his office and let him do simple tasks. He showed his son how to run a business, but he also taught him the importance of character, doing what was right and honest. He once wrote to Pierpont that he should be "very careful with what boys you associate" and only become friends with those "whose influence over you will be good."

When Pierpont was 11 years old, he entered Hartford Public High School. By this time, he had already studied French, German, English, Latin,

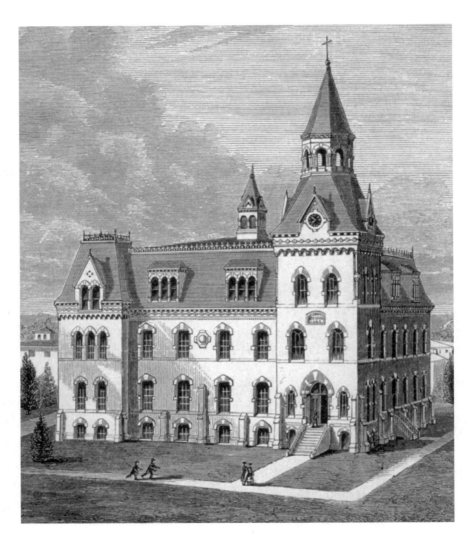

Pierpont attended Hartford Public High School in Hartford, Connecticut.

history, and math. He showed great skill with numbers, although he was better known for fooling around than for studying. He once got thrown out of class for laughing too hard. Upset with this punishment, Pierpont wrote a letter to the teacher.

"I have been treated unjustly," he wrote. He said he would switch to another class if it happened again. Pierpont usually believed he should get his own way. As an adult, his critics would call it arrogance.

At school, Pierpont and his cousin sometimes ventured away from their high school and climbed a tree that hung over a wall at a nearby school for girls. High in the tree, the boys would chat with the girls. Sometimes Pierpont wrote in his diary in secret code about the girls he met. He also noted in his diary when his father traveled and how his business went. He described some of his own activities—"went to dancing school" and "studied Latin." In the winter, he went sledding and skating or stayed indoors and played board games. Pierpont also carefully kept track of letters he sent and received and the money he spent. This attention to detail would be valuable when he entered the business world.

At the age of 14, Pierpont moved with his family to Boston, where he attended a school that focused on math. Now a more serious student, Pierpont enjoyed his classes and did well. But in the spring of 1852, he developed rheumatic fever, a disease that affects the joints of the body. He lost weight, and one of his legs eventually became shorter than the other. To help him recover, his parents sent him to the Azores, a group of islands about 800 miles

(1,280 kilometers) west of Portugal.

Although he was recovering from the fever, Pierpont came down with other illnesses while he was there. But by April 1853, he had fully recovered and regained the weight he had lost. He was 16 years old now, almost 6 feet (180 centimeters) tall, and 150 pounds (67.5 kilograms). Eager to leave the Azores, Pierpont sailed to London, where he stayed for several days on his own. His parents joined him there, and together they traveled throughout Western Europe.

By summer's end, Pierpont was back in Boston preparing for school. During the year, he attended lectures by members of the Whigs, a political party that supported the rapid growth of American businesses. The party was also interested in the issue of slavery. Some Whigs wanted to end slavery completely and immediately, while others only wanted to stop it from spreading to new states or territories. In his diary, Pierpont never gave his opinion about slavery, but he supported most of the Whig policies.

The Whig Party, founded in 1834, generally favored industry and a strong central government. In contrast, the Democrats were populists who favored local government and agriculture. From 1841 to 1853, four of the five U.S. presidents were Whigs, but the party split on the issue of slavery. Antislavery Whigs formed the Republican Party, whose candidate, Abraham Lincoln, was elected president in 1860. Morgan generally supported Republican candidates.

In 1854, Pierpont graduated from high school. Graduating students were required to write an essay about someone they admired. Pierpont wrote about Napoléon Bonaparte, the French general who won many great battles and proclaimed himself emperor of France in 1804. Pierpont wrote that Napoléon was a genius and a man of courage. Years later, some people would compare Morgan to Napoléon. Both were admired because of their unique skills, but both were criticized for how their actions sometimes hurt others.

For now, Pierpont was ready to start his career. Over the next two decades, Pierpont and his father worked together. Junius would arrange business deals, and Pierpont would carry them out. They trusted and cared for each other, although at times they had their differences. ✑

Chapter 3

FIRST BUSINESS DEALS

❧❧❧

In 1854, when Pierpont was 17 years old, his father took a job in London, England, with Peabody & Company. His job was to get the British to invest their money in American businesses. The owner, George Peabody, had already convinced many wealthy British investors to use their money to build American canals, railroads, and banks. When those businesses were successful, the investors shared in their profits.

Soon, Junius' family joined him in London. Pierpont was there just a short time when he went on to Vevey, Switzerland, to continue his education. His father wanted him to improve his French and German. Pierpont also studied math and history.

At Vevey, Pierpont had trouble adjusting to school.

He often ignored the rule to speak only in French, and once he was caught smoking. The head of the school wrote to Junius that Pierpont was "restless at his lessons" and "does not behave well." Over time, Pierpont's behavior and schoolwork improved. He also found time for social activities such as cards, billiards, and dances.

In April 1856, Pierpont left for Göttingen, Germany, where he took classes at the university. The next year, he returned to the United States. "I am anxious to get to work," he wrote. "It seems to me high time." That summer, his father arranged for him to work for Duncan, Sherman & Company, a successful New York bank. One of his duties was to take care of Peabody & Company's operations in the United States.

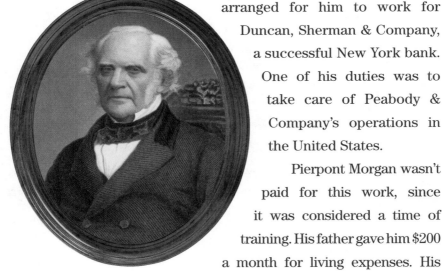

George Peabody (1795–1869), owner of London-based Peabody & Company

Pierpont Morgan wasn't paid for this work, since it was considered a time of training. His father gave him $200 a month for living expenses. His job was meant to sharpen his business skills and help him meet important people. Already, Morgan's future looked bright. He was naturally intelligent and well-educated, spoke several languages, and knew some of the most important leaders in banking. He benefited from belonging to a wealthy family with important connections.

In New York City, Morgan and two roommates lived in a neighborhood of fancy homes. Morgan sometimes walked to his office at the bank, which

Wall Street in New York City became the center for U.S. financial activities in the late 1800s.

was in the financial district not far from the present-day location of the New York Stock Exchange. When he wasn't working, Morgan spent time reading about banking and finance. On weekends, he dined with friends. But one acquaintance said Morgan was not "a party-going young man."

When Morgan started his banking career, many businesses worldwide were in financial trouble. In the United States, railroad companies had spent a lot of money to expand quickly, and now they couldn't pay their bills. The price of grain had fallen, which hurt farmers. A ship carrying more than $1 million in gold sank while sailing from California to the East Coast. Since gold was used as currency, losing the ship affected the nation's finances.

Conditions worsened, and some U.S. banks ran short of money. To increase their money supply, banks demanded that individuals and companies repay their loans immediately. But most of them couldn't do it. In London, Junius Morgan worried that Peabody & Company might fail because it depended on many U.S. companies and banks that were facing financial crises. Morgan wrote his father, "It pained me exceedingly to see how severely the panic now raging on your side [of the ocean] has affected your spirits." Peabody & Company survived, thanks to a loan it received from a British bank. However, the Panic of 1857, as the crisis came to be called, left some Americans out of work for several years.

Since his employer remained stable, Morgan wasn't affected by the panic. He continued to work hard and received a promotion in 1858. He also began investing his money in American companies. When businesses weren't successful, he lost money. When profits were high, Morgan shared in the profits. He was learning how his money, if invested wisely, could make more money.

Amelia "Memie" Sturges

That summer, Morgan became interested in Amelia "Memie" Sturges, the daughter of a wealthy New York investor. Memie left for a while to travel throughout Europe, but when she returned, she and Morgan spent more time together.

Early in 1859, Morgan's job with Duncan, Sherman took

him south. His bank had invested money in cotton, the region's main crop. Morgan's job was to learn more about the cotton business. He spent time on the New Orleans, Louisiana, waterfront, learning from ship captains, who regularly transported goods to ports around the world.

When one captain was having trouble selling a shipment of coffee beans, Morgan told him to charge Duncan, Sherman for them. Then he would try to sell them for a profit. Officials at Duncan, Sherman were

New Orleans, Louisiana, located near the mouth of the Mississippi River, was a center for shipping in the 1800s.

shocked to hear what Morgan had done. After all, he didn't have the authority to make such an important business decision. They told him to get rid of the coffee as fast as he could without losing too much money. Morgan sold the coffee for a profit, which pleased his bosses so much they gave him a share of the earnings. Morgan would remember that sale as his first totally independent business deal.

Although Morgan was eager to hold a paying job, his father wanted him to wait for the right opportunity. Junius thought about sending him to China but instead continued to look for a job for him in New York. In the meantime, Morgan asked Memie to marry him, and they scheduled their wedding for the following year.

The United States was in a crisis at this time. The debate over slavery was dividing the country. When Republican Abraham Lincoln was elected president in November 1860, he assured Southern slave owners that he wouldn't end slavery in the South. His plan was to halt its spread to new territories. Most Southerners, however, thought Lincoln would eventually break his promise and abolish slavery entirely.

In December, South Carolina seceded, or withdrew, from the United States. Soon, six other Southern states left and created the Confederate States of America. President Lincoln declared secession illegal, but in April 1861, four more states seceded and joined the Confederacy. That month, the Civil War began. The South sought independence, while the North used military force to keep the country united.

Morgan didn't share his opinion about the Civil

The Charleston Mercury *newspaper announced the secession of South Carolina from the Union on December 20, 1860.*

CHARLESTON
MERCURY
EXTRA:

Passed unanimously at 1.15 o'clock, P. M., December 20th, 1860.

AN ORDINANCE

To dissolve the Union between the State of South Carolina and other States united with her under the compact entitled " The Constitution of the United States of America."

We, the People of the State of South Carolina, in Convention assembled, do declare and ordain, and it is hereby declared and ordained,

That the Ordinance adopted by us in Convention, on the twenty-third day of May, in the year of our Lord one thousand seven hundred and eighty-eight, whereby the Constitution of the United States of America was ratified, and also, all Acts and parts of Acts of the General Assembly of this State, ratifying amendments of the said Constitution, are hereby repealed; and that the union now subsisting between South Carolina and other States, under the name of "The United States of America," is hereby dissolved.

THE
UNION
IS
DISSOLVED!

shocked to hear what Morgan had done. After all, he didn't have the authority to make such an important business decision. They told him to get rid of the coffee as fast as he could without losing too much money. Morgan sold the coffee for a profit, which pleased his bosses so much they gave him a share of the earnings. Morgan would remember that sale as his first totally independent business deal.

Although Morgan was eager to hold a paying job, his father wanted him to wait for the right opportunity. Junius thought about sending him to China but instead continued to look for a job for him in New York. In the meantime, Morgan asked Memie to marry him, and they scheduled their wedding for the following year.

The United States was in a crisis at this time. The debate over slavery was dividing the country. When Republican Abraham Lincoln was elected president in November 1860, he assured Southern slave owners that he wouldn't end slavery in the South. His plan was to halt its spread to new territories. Most Southerners, however, thought Lincoln would eventually break his promise and abolish slavery entirely.

In December, South Carolina seceded, or withdrew, from the United States. Soon, six other Southern states left and created the Confederate States of America. President Lincoln declared secession illegal, but in April 1861, four more states seceded and joined the Confederacy. That month, the Civil War began. The South sought independence, while the North used military force to keep the country united.

Morgan didn't share his opinion about the Civil

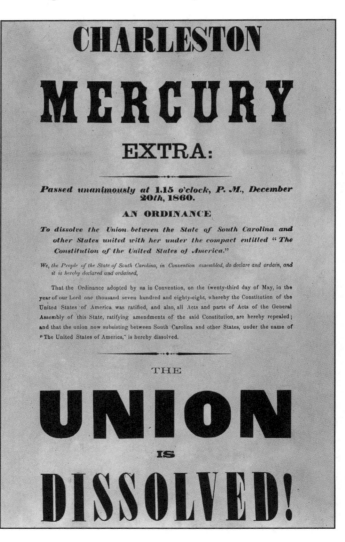

The Charleston Mercury *newspaper announced the secession of South Carolina from the Union on December 20, 1860.*

War, but his father had strong feelings about it. Junius thought the war would hurt U.S. businesses and weaken the country's reputation among world bankers. He called the split between the North and the South "a terrible state of things."

In 1862, Pierpont Morgan left Duncan, Sherman. He rented a one-room office and founded a business called J.P. Morgan & Company. His firm did work for his father and Peabody & Company. That summer, Morgan took part in another business deal that some believe was illegal. A businessman named Stevens planned to buy guns from the U.S. government, improve them, and then sell them back to the government. Morgan loaned Stevens money to buy the guns but then pulled out of the deal. However, Morgan's involvement in the deal later raised questions about his judgment. His critics saw it as war profiteering, or taking advantage of a military crisis to make more profits than normal. Morgan, who had not been careful to learn all the facts, would rarely make that mistake again.

During the Civil War, the U.S. government drafted soldiers. Young men could avoid the draft by paying someone else $300 to take their place. Morgan paid someone the $300 in 1863, because his father wanted him to stay in business. That July, the draft—and the fact that wealthy men like Morgan could avoid it—angered Irish immigrants in New York who opposed the Civil War. This and other issues led the Irish and other immigrants to riot for four days. During the Draft Riots (July 13–16, 1863), as they were called, about 100 people were killed.

Chapter
4 CHANGES AND CHALLENGES

✎⟨∿⟩✎

While the Civil War was raging, Morgan faced many personal challenges. Memie, the woman he wanted to marry, had tuberculosis, a disease that affects the lungs. That didn't stop them from getting married in October 1861. But while they were honeymooning in Europe and North Africa, Memie's condition worsened. In February 1862, just four months after their marriage, she died. Morgan stayed in Europe a few months before returning to New York. Grief-stricken, he threw his energies into his work to take his mind off his wife.

By September, Morgan was exhausted from working so hard. He wrote to his father about the wear and tear he was feeling. To ease his workload, Morgan hired his cousin Jim Goodwin to work with

Twenty-five-year-old J. Pierpont Morgan after the death of his wife Memie in 1862

him, but Morgan still did most of the work. "The fault is with myself only," Morgan said. "When I have a responsibility laid upon me I cannot throw it upon anyone else."

Morgan suffered from headaches and what his doctors called nerves. His stress led to aches, pains, and emotional struggles. Sometimes he battled depression, which had also troubled his mother. Frequent vacations to interesting places around the world often helped him recover from some of his physical and mental ailments.

In spite of his personal problems, Morgan never stopped working. His business had thrived throughout the difficult times of the Civil War. In 1863, he made almost twice as much money as he had the year before. Some of this money came from a deal involving gold.

Morgan and another investor had purchased gold coins and bars worth about $2 million and then shipped half of them to England. This created a gold shortage in America, which made the price of gold go up. Once the price was high enough, Morgan and his partner

Gold is rare and highly prized, which makes it valuable. When trouble threatens, people want gold because it is less likely to lose value. During the Civil War, investors feared that if the North lost, it would not be able to pay its growing debt. Anything that seemed to suggest the North might lose drove up the price of gold. Today, the value of gold still tends to rise when wars break out, as when the United States began its war on terror in 2001.

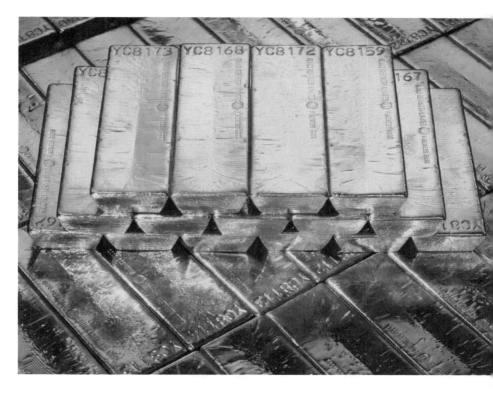

The United States stores most of its gold underground at Fort Knox, Kentucky, and at the Subtreasury in New York City.

brought their gold back from England and sold it for a huge profit. Each man made about $66,000 on the deal.

Morgan often did business by speculation—taking a risk by spending a lot on something whose value might rise quickly. A little bit of speculation helps businesses stay active. Too much, however, can lead to financial problems if values don't go up. For Morgan, speculation paid off. His father, however, thought it was bad business. The risks were too high, Junius said, and money could be lost as easily as it was made.

Junius was angry with his son's gold deal. He told Jim Goodwin that Peabody & Company would no longer do business with J.P. Morgan & Company. Angrily, he wrote to Goodwin, "I have been made most unhappy ... that P. [Pierpont] has so utterly disregarded my warnings."

Peabody & Company didn't cut off its ties with J.P. Morgan & Company after all. But in the fall of 1864, Junius Morgan arranged for his son and Goodwin to work with Charles Dabney, a more experienced banker. The three men created a new company called Dabney, Morgan & Company. By this time, Junius Morgan had taken complete control of the London-based Peabody & Company and changed its name to J.S. Morgan & Company.

Establishing Dabney, Morgan & Company took a lot of Pierpont's time, but he still managed to have a personal life. Toward the end of the year, he became interested in Frances "Fanny" Louise Tracy, the daughter of a well-known and respected lawyer. In March 1865, Morgan asked her to be his wife, and by May, they

Charles W. Dabney

were married. Morgan and his bride went to Europe for their honeymoon.

By that time, the Civil War was nearly over. But the country barely had time to anticipate a peaceful future when President Abraham Lincoln was shot and killed at Ford's Theatre in Washington, D.C. His vice president, Andrew Johnson, became president of the United States. He would begin the difficult task of post-war reconstruction, which meant rebuilding the damage caused by fighting and getting the Southern states back into the Union.

Frances "Fanny" Louise Tracy Morgan, second wife of J. Pierpont Morgan

Morgan never said or wrote much about national events. But he always supported politicians and policies that favored investors like him. One of the policies he backed was getting rid of the paper money the government had issued during the war. Morgan wanted hard currency—gold—as the country's system of money. He believed that foreign investors would stop investing in the U.S. government or American companies if their profits weren't paid in gold. Morgan was convinced that the country needed

During the Civil War, the U.S. government printed so many greenbacks, or paper money, that they amounted to more than the gold the government held in reserve.

foreign investors' money in order to keep growing. Although the government didn't get rid of paper money, called gold certificates, a person could now redeem them for gold.

In March 1866, Morgan and his wife Fanny had their first child, a daughter named Louisa. Eighteen months later, John Pierpont Morgan Jr. was born. They called him Jack. Their family was growing, but Morgan and his wife were often apart. Fanny preferred the countryside to New York City and sometimes left the city to recover from bouts of depression. At times, Morgan went to Saratoga Springs, New York, to improve his own health. But Morgan preferred living in the bustling city near his business or traveling to other continents.

During the summer of 1868, he traveled throughout Europe without his family. A pattern was starting that would grow more noticeable over the years. Morgan preferred to travel alone or with several companions, but usually not with Fanny.

In the summer of 1869, Morgan and Fanny did travel together. The first transcontinental railway had just been completed, connecting the Eastern United States to California. Morgan wanted to ride the train to visit the Western states. The trip was partly a vacation and partly a chance for him to study the condition of the nation's railroads. Most of Dabney, Morgan & Company's money financed railroad companies. When Morgan returned to New York in September, railroads dominated his affairs.

Earlier that year, Morgan's company had loaned money to the Albany and Susquehanna (A&S), a small New York railway. It connected to four major railways that went to Pennsylvania. One of the railroad companies was owned by Jay Gould, an investor later known for his ruthless deals. Gould and a man named James Fisk wanted to take control of the recently completed A&S.

Resisting them was Joseph

> The first public railroad in the United States opened six years before J. Pierpont Morgan was born. Until then, most people traveled on foot, on horseback, or in wagons or canal boats pulled by animals. The arrival of steam-powered trains made it easier to transport people and goods long distances. The growth of railroads was centered in the Northeast. Slowly, more tracks were laid in the Midwest, the South, and the West. By 1860, the United States had about 30,000 miles (48,000 km) of railroad tracks, and railroad companies were the largest businesses in the country.

In a railroad riot in Binghamton, New York, over control of the Albany & Susquehanna Railroad, locomotives were used as weapons of assault.

Ramsey, founder and president of the A&S. Fisk and Gould insisted on taking over the A&S, which led to a violent clash between the two sides near Binghamton, New York. One magazine writer reported, "Pistols were used, with stones, clubs, and fists."

Morgan came to Ramsey's aid and invested money in the A&S Railroad. This gave the A&S money to

grow and, at the same time, allowed Morgan to share in the profits. Morgan also attended the company's annual meeting, where he spoke up for the group that didn't want Gould to take over the railway. The company appreciated what he had done and elected him vice president.

To prevent Gould from attempting to take control of the company again, Morgan leased the A&S to another railroad. Now the railroad was out of Gould's reach. The A&S deal would often be called a railroad war, and Morgan's actions would be referred to as a rescue.

In 1873, *The New York Times* newspaper reported that Morgan's victory with the A&S "made Mr. Morgan universally regarded as an able financier," someone skilled in financial matters. Morgan would find himself in other business battles in the years to come. He would usually come out a winner. ✍

5 THE GOOD TIMES AND THE BAD

❦

At the beginning of the A&S Railroad war, Morgan had moved with Fanny and the children to a new home in New York City. Fanny gave birth to a daughter named Juliet in 1870 and to another child, Anne, in 1873.

Although Morgan concentrated mostly on business, he still took breaks to travel to Europe and Africa to collect books, paintings, and rare art objects. His interest in ancient artifacts motivated him to help establish the American Museum of Natural History in 1869. Two years later, Morgan donated $1,000 to start an art museum that would be called the Metropolitan Museum of Art. Morgan's interest in art would continue to grow in the years to come.

Morgan was enjoying his trips, but he was not entirely happy with his work. Charles Dabney was

Four of the Morgan children (from left): Jack, Anne, Louisa, and Juliet

about to retire, and Morgan was having trouble with a new partner who had just joined the firm. The stress at work was causing him health problems. At the beginning of 1871, he informed his father that he wanted to quit Dabney, Morgan & Company. His father soon had a new business proposal for him and told him to meet with a Philadelphia, Pennsylvania, financier named Anthony Drexel.

In March, Morgan visited Drexel at his home. Drexel knew of Morgan's financial talents and his connection to London banking. He asked Morgan to become a partner in his Philadelphia company and lead a new banking firm in New York. It would be called Drexel, Morgan & Company.

On an old envelope, Drexel scribbled his offer. Morgan took the envelope back to New York to discuss the idea with his father. Junius approved, and Pierpont Morgan took control of the new company, a much larger and stronger company than Dabney, Morgan & Company.

Before settling down in his new position, Morgan took another long vacation. For more than a year, he traveled throughout Europe with Fanny and the children. They also visited Egypt, where they sailed up the Nile River and visited ancient sites, including the pyramids that were built around 2500 B.C. Morgan developed a fascination with Egypt and its history. He would return many times during his lifetime.

Morgan visited the Temple of Horus at Edfu, Egypt.

When the Morgans returned to the United States in the fall of 1872, they moved into yet another new home in Highland Falls, New York. The estate, called

Cragston, included a large house, horse stables, dog kennels, tennis courts, and more than 300 acres (121 hectares) of land along the Hudson River. When Morgan stayed at Cragston, he traveled to work in New York City by steamboat. He often stayed at the home he still owned in New York City. Cragston became his country estate where he escaped city life and visited his family from time to time.

Morgan continued to pay close attention to the Morgan companies, which collectively were known as the House of Morgan. But he also focused on how the U.S. economy was doing. In 1873, he heard rumblings that the railroad industry was in trouble. Some investors were afraid they might lose large amounts of money.

Business had been booming in the United States since the end of the Civil War in 1865. Railroad companies had built thousands of miles of railroad tracks. Bankers and wealthy people had invested lots of money in the railroad industry. But now, the U.S. economy was showing signs of weakness.

Railroads had overbuilt. There were too many tracks and not enough companies willing or able to use them. This especially affected a business called Jay Cooke & Company, which had invested heavily in a transcontinental railway called the Northern Pacific. Jay Cooke realized too late that he had spent too much money. By September 1873, the railroad

The transcontinental Northern Pacific Railroad

company was bankrupt—out of money.

Other companies had also overspent. People stopped investing in those companies. The New York Stock Exchange, where investors buy and sell shares in companies, closed for 10 days. Banks demanded that investors pay back their loans immediately. Investors tried to sell their shares quickly at a very low price in order to pay their debts. Because companies were receiving less money from investors, they could no longer afford all their employees, and they began firing workers. These events that affected the whole country came to be called the Panic of 1873.

A crowd mobs Broad Street near the New York Stock Exchange in New York City during the financial Panic of 1873.

The day after Jay Cooke & Company went bankrupt, Morgan sent a telegram to his father in London. "Affairs continue unprecedented [exceptionally] bad, large failures," he wired. However, about Drexel, Morgan & Company, he wrote, "Everything satisfactory with us." But there was tension at the office.

Morgan had forced some struggling investors to pay off their loans with Drexel, Morgan & Company. Joseph Drexel, one of the firm's partners, hadn't wanted to demand payment of the loans. Morgan, in turn, didn't think Drexel was a good businessman. Within two years Drexel left the company.

Morgan's decision to demand repayment of some loans kept Drexel, Morgan & Company financially strong. From then on, Morgan told his father, he would deal only with what "can be recommended without a shadow of doubt." Morgan was a careful investor. As a result, he seldom lost large amounts of money in risky financial deals.

The Panic of 1873 happened in part because there was no U.S. central bank—no national supply of money. President Ulysses S. Grant had no way to help banks that were running out of money, so the House of Morgan stepped in to help. The Morgan banking firms loaned money to banks and convinced British investors to put money into American banks and companies. Still, the U.S. economy remained weak for several years. People across the nation lost their jobs, and investors lost millions of dollars. Through it all, Drexel, Morgan & Company weathered the financial storms well.

Today, the Federal Reserve System serves as the nation's central bank. Panics like the one in 1873 occurred largely because there was no way to manage the nation's money and economy. The charter of the first Bank of the United States, created by Alexander Hamilton in 1791, was allowed to expire in 1811. A second U.S. bank was established in 1816, but President Andrew Jackson vetoed its renewal in 1836. It was not until 1913 that the U.S. Federal Reserve System was created.

There is a difference
between an economic
panic and a recession
or depression. A panic
is generally short-lived
and is often limited
to financial institutions,
such as banks. A reces-
sion is longer and
affects many industries,
causing higher unem-
ployment or cuts in
workers' wages. A
depression is a particu-
larly long recession.
The worst and most
famous depression in
the United States was
the Great Depression
of the 1930s.

In 1875, Morgan was suffering again from bouts of depression. Usually he got through these times by working very hard or traveling. But this time, he thought about not going back to work and leaving the business world. Junius Morgan stepped in, however, and told his son to carry on.

Morgan's wife, Fanny, was also experiencing times of melancholy and gloominess. She had become antisocial and seemed content to isolate herself from her husband and society. She spent most of her time at home and visited only with her children. By the mid-1870s, Morgan and Fanny's relationship had deteriorated, and they hardly saw each other.

At times, Morgan wrote letters to Fanny that expressed how much he loved her. But at other times, he found it hard to share his feelings with her. He wrote that mistakes with words "throw me into such a state of depression that I get quite exhausted and after I have written I am completely used up and unfit for anything for hours."

Fanny and Pierpont would continue to grow

further apart in the years to come. Although they stayed married, Morgan had relationships with other women who eagerly spent time with him and enjoyed his company and his wealth.

Morgan finally threw himself back into his work, but only after another long vacation to Europe and Egypt. When he returned to New York in 1877, he made a deal with the U.S. government. Congress had not given the U.S. War Department enough money to pay soldiers' wages. Morgan loaned the government money and agreed not to charge any interest. He made the deal on his own without getting advice from his father. Although he had good relations with his father and trusted his suggestions, 40-year-old Morgan sometimes made independent decisions. Many of these decisions would bring large profits to the House of Morgan. ❧

J. Pierpont Morgan at the age of 44

6 SPENDING AND GIVING

❦

Although Drexel, Morgan & Company's main business was financing railroads, Morgan was open to new ideas and opportunities. In 1878, Egisto Fabbri, one of his partners, talked eagerly about a young man and his amazing inventions. Thomas Edison of Menlo Park, New Jersey, had recently invented a device called the phonograph. He was also developing an electric lightbulb that could burn for many hours. The bulb still needed more work, and Edison needed money to perfect it.

Fabbri invested in Edison's company, the Edison Electric Light Company. Drexel, Morgan & Company became the company's bank. Eventually, Morgan would also invest personally in Edison's company. Edison believed his connection to the House of

Morgan's study at his home at 219 Madison Ave. in New York City was illuminated by Edison's electrical lightbulbs.

Morgan would ensure his company's success.

Edison was also trying to create a system that would supply electricity to entire cities. Some people, including Junius Morgan, didn't think the inventor would succeed. But Pierpont Morgan was confident that the improved lightbulb and an electrical system to put them along streets and in homes and businesses would be a good investment. He wrote to a friend, "I think there is a good thing in this for parties [people] who ... introduce it properly to cities."

With money from investors like Morgan and Fabbri, Edison built an electric power station on Pearl Street in New York City. In 1882, Drexel, Morgan & Company had electric lights installed in its office, thus becoming the first business customer of Edison Electric Light Company. A small power plant was installed at Morgan's home on Madison Avenue to supply power for lights throughout his house.

Thomas Alva Edison (1847–1931) was often called the Wizard of Menlo Park. His inventions helped create the recorded music and film industries. His research and inventions made electricity common in buildings and homes. Although the first lightbulb was invented by English inventor Joseph Swan, Edison did create an improved bulb that burned much longer.

Many guests visited Morgan's home to see Edison's wonderful invention. A reporter wrote, "Mr. Morgan's house is distinguished for being the first private dwelling in New York City in which the Edison

Thomas Alva Edison and his original electric power station called a dynamo

electric light has been successfully introduced." Morgan's home became a showcase for Edison's invention. The house was much larger than any others Morgan owned. It featured an elevator, a gym for children, and an enormous bulletproof safe. A telegraph wire connected his house to his office. Morgan could certainly afford this lavish house. He was now earning between $500,000 and $1 million per year at Drexel, Morgan & Company. Money from investments added to his vast riches.

Morgan enjoyed decorating his home with

paintings by European and American artists. He collected ancient ceramics, old books, and letters, a hobby he shared with his father. Some of his treasures included four original letters written by George Washington and original autographs of all the signers of the Declaration of Independence.

Collecting art and artifacts wasn't Morgan's only expensive hobby. Like other wealthy men of the era, he enjoyed sailing on extravagant yachts. He bought his first yacht, the *Corsair*, in 1882. Inside was a tiled fireplace and silk-covered furniture. When asked how much it cost to buy and operate a yacht like the *Corsair*, Morgan had several responses. He often said, "If you have to ask, you can't afford it."

Not all of Morgan's personal interests involved

A 1922 photograph of Morgan's yacht, the Corsair

spending money on himself. He was also a great philanthropist who gave time and money to organizations and churches like St. George's Episcopal Church in New York City. Morgan had strong religious beliefs and thought only faith in Jesus Christ would help a person get to heaven. He didn't think people could buy their way into heaven by doing good deeds or giving away money. Still, he gave hundreds of thousands of dollars to the church and supported its mission to help the poor.

His generosity even extended to the Episcopal priest. Morgan helped bring the Reverend William Rainsford from Ireland to New York in 1883. During their 30-year friendship, Morgan helped support Rainsford's family and bought them a home. As his wealth increased, Morgan continued to spend money to help others but didn't hesitate to buy the fine things he could easily afford for himself.

At the same time, Morgan continued to have health problems and suffer from more bouts of depression. In the 1880s, he developed rhinophyma, a condition that causes a person's nose to turn red, get larger, and become misshapen. At times, Morgan seemed embarrassed about the condition, but he didn't seek help to correct it. Later in his life, his nose was almost as famous as he was. He said, "Everybody knows my nose and it would be impossible for me to appear on the streets of New York without it." ஐ

Chapter
7   IN COMMAND

❦⟋⟍❦

Throughout the 1880s, the Morgan companies remained strong and kept up good reputations as some of the world's greatest banking firms. The New York office of Drexel, Morgan & Company was making some important deals. In London, J.S. Morgan & Company also continued to handle important matters. But things were changing within the House of Morgan. Junius Morgan, now in his 70s, was often sick. Leadership in the House of Morgan was shifting to Pierpont Morgan.

Railroads were still Morgan's main focus, and by 1880, the railroad industry was booming. About 70,000 miles (112,000 km) of track had been built across the United States. Over the next 10 years, an additional 84,000 miles (134,400 km) of track would be built. In

In the 1880s, railroad companies like the New York Central and the Hudson River grew rapidly.

no other decade would U.S. railroad companies lay that much track. By 1900, the United States would have 193,000 miles (308,800 km) of railroad tracks. Railroad companies were growing fast, and Morgan took advantage of it.

Industrialist William Henry Vanderbilt (1821–1885)

At the end of 1879, a wealthy businessman named William Vanderbilt decided to sell most of his shares in the New York Central Railroad. It was one of the largest railroads in the East and had been built by his father, Cornelius. Vanderbilt did not want to sell all of his shares at once. He asked Morgan if Drexel, Morgan & Company would buy 250,000 shares and then resell them to investors. Morgan arranged for a number of banks and investors, including Jay Gould, to buy some of the shares and either keep them or resell them. J.S. Morgan & Company bought the most shares, about 40,000, but the rest were sold mainly to American companies.

The New York Central Railroad didn't provide the public with much information about its financial situation. Investors had to trust Morgan when he told them that the shares were worth what the railroad was asking: $120 each. At first, sales were slow. The railroad company dropped the price to increase sales, but Morgan was confident the price would go back up. He told one business associate, "Don't you sell any shares. I know what I'm talking about; it is going up much higher." Morgan was right. The price went up, and investors made a nice profit.

As part of the deal, Morgan demanded to be a member of the railroad's board of directors. That way, he would have more control over the railroad company's financial decisions and future business deals.

Other railroad companies were trying to drive their competitors out of business by lowering ticket prices. The New York Central Railroad and its competitor, the Pennsylvania Railroad, kept charging less and less, hoping to lure more customers. But lower prices meant less profit for investors. Morgan wanted to end these so-called railroad wars and keep profits high.

Jay Gould is often called one of the robber barons of the 19th century. Others included Cornelius Vanderbilt and John D. Rockefeller. Robber barons were powerful investors criticized for placing their own drive for wealth above the laws and interests of the country. One businessman called Gould "the worst man on earth since the beginning of the Christian era." Others argue that Gould improved the companies he took over, which helped workers and other investors.

In 1884, the Pennsylvania Railroad bought a smaller railroad company that had gone bankrupt. The newly acquired tracks ran alongside a main route of the New York Central Railroad. The owners of the Pennsylvania Railroad hoped to give the New York Central some stiff competition.

At the same time, the Pennsylvania Railroad was facing competition from a small railroad with connections to New York Central. The budding war between these two major railroads was sure to cause big problems. Morgan decided to end what he called an absurd struggle.

In July 1885, he invited the presidents of the two railroads to meet on his yacht. As they sailed along the Hudson River, Morgan explained the situation to the two men. Railroad wars made foreign banks less likely to invest in U.S. railroads, he explained. If the two companies didn't end their struggle, the flow of money would stop.

The president of New York Central Railroad had a plan. His

Although Morgan disliked competition among the railroad companies, many Americans disagreed. They liked the low prices that resulted from strong competition. To promote competition, Congress passed the Interstate Commerce Act in 1887. The law created the Interstate Commerce Commission (ICC), the first government body designed to regulate the actions of a U.S. industry. At first, the ICC only dealt with railroads, but later it regulated other industries. Government agencies still exist today to regulate U.S. businesses and industries.

company would take control of the railway that the
Pennsylvania Railroad had just bought. In return,
New York Central would turn over the small railroad
that was taking business away from the Pennsylvania
Railroad. The president of the Pennsylvania Railroad
agreed.

Soon, the price of railroad stock began to rise,
and newspapers praised Morgan for ending a costly
railroad war. Junius Morgan also added his approval,
saying his son "handled the ... affair better than I could
have done it myself." However, the kind of deal the

*An 1880s car-
toon depicts
railroad owners
dividing up
America and
trying to take
control of
U.S. railways.*

two railroad companies made would later be called collusion and would become illegal. New laws would support more competition.

During the next several years, Morgan continued to help end disagreements in the railroad industry. He helped create an association of railway owners to try to keep peace. The group folded, however, when it couldn't agree with some of the railroad companies in the West.

By 1890, J. Pierpont Morgan was a well-known financier and the most important banker in the United States. Seventy-seven-year-old Junius Morgan had come to completely trust his son's judgment. However, that spring, a tragedy struck the Morgan family. In April, while on a horse-drawn carriage ride through the countryside of France, Junius Morgan fell out of his carriage when a passing train startled the horses. His head struck a stone wall, and within two days, he was dead.

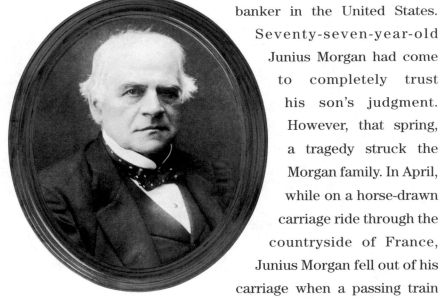

Junius Spencer Morgan died at the age of 77.

When the accident happened, Pierpont was on his way to England. By the time he reached Liverpool, his father had already died. When he received the bad news, he headed immediately to France. His father had always been very important to him and had helped him become a great success. Although they had had their differences throughout the years and Junius could sometimes be overly demanding of his son, Pierpont was grief-stricken about his death. One of Morgan's friends described his sorrow as "deep, almost uncontrollable."

Junius' body was brought back to Hartford for the funeral and burial. After Morgan had laid his father to rest, he immediately went back to work. He was now head of Drexel, Morgan & Company as well as J.S. Morgan & Company. And he was head of the powerful House of Morgan.

J. Pierpont Morgan was also one of the richest men in the United States. Junius Morgan had left his son an estate worth $15 million, an amount equivalent to more than $225 million today. ☙

FACTORY
GARNEKIE & KANE

TRUSTS ARE LARGELY PRIVATE AFFAIRS WITH WHICH NEITHER PRESIDENT CLEVELAND NOR ANY PRIVATE CITIZEN HAS ANY PARTICULAR RIGHT TO INTERFERE
JAMES G. BLAINE

Chapter

8 TIME OF CRISIS

⤦⤧⤦

The late 19th century in the United States was aptly called the Gilded Age. Gilt is a metal with a thin layer of gold on top, but underneath, it lacks value. Some Americans thought the U.S. economy was like gilt. On the surface, the country seemed incredibly wealthy. Millionaires like J. Pierpont Morgan, Charles Schwab, Andrew Carnegie, and William Vanderbilt were incredibly successful. But underneath, hundreds of thousands of Americans faced poverty, terrible working conditions, and unemployment.

Since the 1870s, U.S. politics had been shaped largely by two competing forces. On one side were financiers and industrialists who opposed any government efforts to control how they ran their huge businesses. They wanted to keep the gold standard—

Lithograph of a distressed family resting outside a factory door during the depression of 1893

money was either made out of gold or could be traded in for gold. Morgan supported the gold standard, and like most people with these views, he supported the Republican Party.

On the other side were farmers, small business owners, and workers. They wanted the government to limit the power of big business and railroads. They disliked the gold standard, because the supply of gold was limited. They thought silver should also be used as currency. They argued that silver was more plentiful, so there would be more money for common people. It would be easier for people to pay back their debts. Some Democrats held these views, but people called Populists were the main supporters of this idea that was called free silver.

Congress had already made gold the sole standard for currency in 1873. But by 1890, the country was bimetallic, which meant that both gold and silver were used for currency. Three years later, the country was in an economic depression. Many people were losing their jobs. Others demanded higher wages to keep up with the high cost of living.

President Grover Cleveland blamed the crisis on bimetallic currency. He convinced Congress to put the country back on the gold standard. Populists blamed the problem on the government for not issuing as much silver money as it should have. The money debate over whether to use gold or silver was

dividing the country.

Although Cleveland was a Democrat, Morgan clearly backed his actions. Using a bimetallic stan-

Farmers opposed big business and wanted more money for common people.

69

The Populists traced their roots back to the 1870s, when U.S. farmers in Western and Southern states first protested high railroad prices. In 1891, the Populists formed their own political party and nominated a candidate for president. The Populists wanted many things that were considered radical at the time. They wanted an income tax, and they thought the government should own certain types of businesses. Although most Populists were farmers, they tried to win the support of factory workers by calling for a shorter workweek. To Populists, Morgan and others like him stood for everything they thought was wrong with the United States: too much money and power in the hands of too few people.

dard had lowered the value of the U.S. dollar when it was compared to other currencies around the world. Foreign investors were afraid their money wouldn't be worth much in the United States. They cashed in their paper money for gold and took it out of the United States.

Even after Cleveland got rid of silver currency, people continued to take gold out of the country. The U.S. government had stored $100 million in gold, but investors thought the government would one day run out of it. They took their gold while they could.

As the depression of 1893 got worse, many railroad companies went out of business. Other businesses were also in trouble. A New York newspaper noted, "Mills, factories, furnaces nearly everywhere shut down in large numbers." By 1894, as many as 20 percent of workers didn't have jobs. The government's gold reserve had fallen well below $100 million. The United States would have to

buy or borrow gold from other countries to bring the gold reserve back up. President Cleveland turned to businesses, banks, and J. Pierpont Morgan for help.

Twice in 1894, Morgan and other bankers invested money in the United States so the government could

A railroad building in Chicago, Illinois, was closed during the depression of 1893.

71

buy gold. Each time, the gold reserve briefly went up to a healthy level, and then it plunged again. Investors were still taking gold out of the country. By early 1895, the gold reserve was decreasing by $2 million a day. At that rate, it would soon run out.

Cleveland was running out of options for ending the crisis. The free-silver supporters were demanding a return to the bimetallic standard. Millions of people were still out of work. Morgan thought the only solution was to get Europeans to invest their money in the U.S. government.

By now, Congress was getting impatient with Cleveland. Many members wanted to go back to using silver. The president's advisers met with Morgan several times. In February, Morgan went to Washington, D.C. to meet with Cleveland face-to-face. The situation was critical to the House of Morgan and its customers. Morgan said, "We all have large interests dependent upon maintenance [keeping] sound currency."

On February 5, 1895, Morgan and two of his

Grover Cleveland (1837–1908) was president of the United States from 1885 to 1889 and from 1893 to 1897.

banking partners met with Cleveland. In the White House, the bankers sat in a corner of the president's office while Cleveland talked with several aides. As Morgan rolled an unlit cigar in his hands, the president received bad news that the supply of gold was dropping drastically. Cleveland turned to Morgan and asked if he had any suggestions.

Morgan described his plan. A group of bankers in the United States and London would keep up to $100 million in gold on reserve for the U.S. government. The gold would be considered a loan and would

Railroads, coal and iron mines, steel plants, and electrical power stations were established during what came to be called the Industrial Era.

not leave the country. Morgan assured the president that he had the cooperation of the other bankers and the power to keep the gold in the country for at least six months. In return, the bankers would receive U.S. bonds, or written promises that the government would repay the debt.

The meeting lasted four and a half hours. Cleveland wanted the details kept secret, since Congress was still working on a separate plan. However, no one expected that plan to be approved. Cleveland didn't want Congress or the rest of the country to know he had worked out a private deal with Morgan.

Later that day, a happy Morgan sent a message back to his New York office. "We have carried our point & are more than satisfied." Congress, as expected, rejected the plan they were working on, and on February 8, 1895, Cleveland announced the deal with Morgan. Morgan's group of bankers reserved $65 million in gold for the government. The deal was a success for Morgan, and it saved the country from financial collapse.

Still, the secret deal upset some Americans. They thought big business was making huge profits while most people were without jobs and money. The following year, Congress investigated the deal and asked Morgan to answer some questions. Morgan argued that the entire U.S. financial system would

have collapsed if he had not acted. "I had no object except to save the disaster that would result in case ... foreign gold had not been obtained."

Throughout his career, Morgan thought his interests and the country's interests were very similar. He believed that what helped him also helped the country. Saving the gold reserve, he said, was an example of this. But in the years to come, more Americans would doubt his lofty words. ❧

A cartoon of Morgan helping Uncle Sam showed how Morgan had brought the U.S. government out of financial difficulties several times.

9 BIG BUSINESS

Chapter

❧⟳❧

During the gold crisis, changes were taking place within the House of Morgan. In early 1895, Morgan changed the name of his banking firm from Drexel, Morgan & Company to J.P. Morgan & Company. As the leading financial backer of U.S. railroads, Morgan's company now had a large say in how railroad companies ran their businesses. He was also involved in several mergers.

In the 1890s, industries that made similar products sometimes merged to form one large company. Morgan realized that these combinations, called trusts, made higher profits than several smaller companies could. The House of Morgan helped form several of these trusts. In 1892, Morgan helped create General Electric from two competing

The headquarters of J.P. Morgan & Company was located at the corner of Wall Street and Broad Street in New York City.

Trusts began forming in the 1880s. People traded their shares in small companies for part ownership in trusts, large businesses made up of several smaller companies. Trusts appeared in many industries, including sugar, oil, copper, and rubber. They could set high prices for their goods, since consumers couldn't get the products anywhere else. Some Americans feared the economic power of the trusts and large companies, so Congress passed several antitrust laws. They still apply today. In 2000, Microsoft, the immense computer software company, was found guilty of breaking antitrust laws. The company was forced to share some of its private information with its competitors.

electric companies: Edison Electric Company and Thomson-Houston Company. In 1898, he helped form a leading steel trust called Federal Steel. Morgan's goal was to limit competition and ensure that the companies made high profits.

Morgan was also making hefty profits for himself. By the end of the 1890s, he was earning an average of more than $2 million per year, which didn't include what he made on his personal investments. Morgan didn't hesitate to spend his profits. He bought a home in Newport, Rhode Island; an apartment on Jekyll Island off the coast of Georgia; and a mountain home in northern New York state. The New York property, called Camp Uncas, included 1,500 acres (600 hectares) of land and its own sugarhouse, where sap from maple trees was turned into maple syrup. Although Camp Uncas was deep in the woods, Morgan brought in many of the comforts of city life like modern bathrooms, telephone lines, and two pianos.

Morgan's wife Fanny didn't share the new homes with her husband, and they rarely saw each other. Throughout much of the 1890s, Morgan spent time with a woman named Adelaide Douglas. She was one of several women with whom he had relationships during the latter part of his life. He was generous with Adelaide, buying her jewelry, art, antiques, clothing, and a house.

Morgan's home at Newport, Rhode Island

Morgan lived most of his life in New York City and traveled extensively in Europe and Africa.

Morgan also took a greater interest in yachting. In 1897, he was named commodore, or head, of the New York Yacht Club. In 1899, he led the yacht club's efforts to build a yacht, the *Columbia*, that would compete in the America's Cup yacht race. That year, the *Columbia* defeated its British challenger. A New York newspaper reported that after the victory, Commodore Morgan gave "a shout of delight ... and danced about with joy."

At work, Morgan continued to assert his power and influence. In February 1901, he purchased Carnegie Steel Company from Andrew Carnegie and merged it with Federal Steel to create the gigantic U.S. Steel Corporation. The merger created a buzz in America and Europe. Many people saw the huge company as a threat to other steel companies and their workers. One London paper said U.S. Steel was "a menace to the commerce of the civilized world."

Soon after the deal, as Morgan was vacationing in Europe, he received disturbing news. The owner of the Union Pacific Railroad and some powerful investors were trying to take control of the Northern Pacific by buying up most of the company's shares. Morgan ordered his partners to buy Northern Pacific stock before the Union Pacific could take control. He was willing to pay any price to get the shares and stop the Union Pacific from gaining control.

Morgan's group was successful, and the value of Northern Pacific stock soared. Other investors began putting their money in Northern Pacific so they too could share in the profits. The price per share continued to climb, while the price of other companies' stock fell.

As a result, a panic hit Wall Street. *The New York Times* wrote that "brokers acted like insane men" as they tried to sell other companies' shares and buy shares of Northern Pacific. Morgan didn't feel guilty about starting the panic. He believed his duty was to protect companies like Northern Pacific. Later that year, the Northern Pacific Railroad became even stronger by merging with four other railroad companies to form a trust called Northern Securities Company.

Theodore Roosevelt (1858–1919) was the 26th president of the United States.

In September 1901, Republican Vice President Theodore Roosevelt became president of the United States when President William McKinley was assassinated. Morgan had known the president's father and supported Roosevelt when he was a New York politician. Now, however, the two men had very different views on business. Roosevelt thought business trusts were gaining too much power. Early in 1902, the Roosevelt administration brought the Northern Securities Company to court. Roosevelt believed the company was violating antitrust laws that had been passed in 1873 to prevent businesses from dominating one type of industry and getting most of the profits. Morgan headed to Washington, D.C., to talk to Roosevelt. He wanted the president to cancel the lawsuit, but Roosevelt firmly said no. Morgan asked, "Are you going to attack my other interests?" Roosevelt replied, "Certainly not—unless we find out ... that they have done something that we regard as wrong."

The Northern Securities case was tried in Minnesota where the company was based. At the end of the trial, the judge ordered the group of railroad companies to split. Northern Securities appealed to the U.S. Supreme Court, the highest court in the country. But the Supreme Court agreed with the Minnesota court: Northern Securities had broken the law. Supreme Court Justice John Marshall Harlan wrote, "No combination, however powerful, is stronger than the law." Morgan was entering a time when the U.S. government would increasingly question large companies and how they did business.

Despite Morgan's troubles with Roosevelt, the two men worked together on other issues. About 150,000 coal miners in western Pennsylvania went on strike in 1902. They refused to work unless they received better pay and an eight-hour workday. Violence broke out between the strikers and local police. The price of coal began to rise as fewer workers were mining less coal. Public outcries against the strike forced Roosevelt to take action.

Most of the coal mines were owned by railroad companies under Morgan's control. Roosevelt turned to Morgan for assistance and asked him to help end the strike. Morgan and one of Roosevelt's advisers worked on a solution. They came up with a deal that gave miners some of the things they demanded. Then Morgan convinced the presidents of the railroad companies to accept the deal, and the coal miners went back to work. Roosevelt thanked Morgan in a letter:

> *If it had not been for your going into the matter I do not see how the strike could have been settled at this time.*

People lined up to buy coal, which was scarce during the coal strike of 1902.

Some people thought Morgan was a hero for helping his country and big business. Others were leery of him and thought his huge trusts were making too much profit. But few people really knew Morgan. He rarely spoke to reporters, and his blunt way of doing business hid the fact that he was actually quite a shy man.

But there was no denying his power. When trouble would once again hit the U.S. economy in 1907, Morgan would be ready to step in. ✑

10 THE BIG CHIEF

Chapter

❧❀❧

In 1907, J. Pierpont Morgan turned 70 and spent the summer traveling throughout Europe. His 40-year-old son, Jack, who had worked for his father for 15 years, now had a leadership role at J.P. Morgan & Company. He kept his father up-to-date on what was going on and informed him if a crisis arose.

For some time, the U.S. economy had shown signs of weakness. Speculation was running wild as individuals and businesses bought up shares in mining and railroad companies. President Roosevelt was still criticizing the trusts and wealthy men like Morgan who created them. Investors were afraid the president would try to split up the trusts. Life insurance companies had typically invested heavily in American companies, but now they began to cut

J. Pierpont Morgan with his son, Jack (John Pierpont Morgan Jr.)

back. Investors were again taking gold out of the country. This spelled trouble for the U.S. economy.

In October 1907, stock prices fell sharply, and some banks began to fail. If a bank failed, people who had deposited their money there had little chance of ever seeing it again. One observer noted that New York was in the middle of "a financial and banking disaster such as none of us had ever experienced."

"They are in trouble in New York," Morgan told a friend. "They do not know what to do, and I don't know what to do, but I am going back." Morgan returned to the United States and worked on a solution to the crisis. He formed a small group that decided which failing banks would receive help from the House of Morgan and other powerful banks.

Morgan arranged for a $3 million loan to the Trust Company of America, the second largest trust in New York City. John D. Rockefeller, a wealthy financier, loaned the trust $10 million and announced his support of Morgan. The next day, Morgan made a $10 million loan to the New York Stock Exchange to keep it operating. From his office on Wall Street, Morgan heard cheers erupt as stockbrokers found out. Other companies also gave large amounts of money to save the New York Stock Exchange. Less than a week later, Morgan loaned money to the city of New York so it could pay its bills. One banker later wrote, "Probably no one could have got the banks to act together ... as he [Morgan] did."

Once again, Morgan received both praise and criticism for his actions. His admirers said he had prevented an economic disaster. Others blamed him and other financiers for creating the panic in the first place. As always, Morgan believed he had taken the right steps to help his country through a dangerous time. He seemed pleased when he rode through New York and heard people on the street say, "There goes the Big Chief!"

Trading on the floor of the New York Stock Exchange

The Panic of 1907 led to changes in U.S. banking. Many Americans didn't want the country to rely on private banks during future financial troubles. As one U.S. senator said, "We may not always have Pierpont Morgan with us to meet a banking crisis." In 1913, Congress created the Federal Reserve System, which has 12 government banks scattered throughout the country. In charge of the Fed, as it is called, is a board of governors chosen by the president, with the approval of the U.S. Senate. The United States still uses this system today.

Halting the Panic of 1907, as it was called, was Morgan's last great public act. Now he spent even more time traveling and collecting art. Some claimed he had already spent $60 million on his growing collection of expensive paintings and art objects. He kept most of the items in London and gave some away to avoid paying U.S. taxes on them. But in 1911, Congress changed the laws, which made it less costly for Morgan to bring the art to the United States.

Morgan's collection was so large that he built a private library at his New York home on Madison Avenue to house it. Among his books was a copy of *Aesop's Fables* dated 1476 and a 1455 Gutenberg Bible, the first book printed on the printing press. With 30-foot (9-m) ceilings and walls decorated with expensive art, the library was a symbol of Morgan's lavish wealth.

But Morgan's attention was still on business and politics. In 1908, William Howard Taft was elected president of the United States. Taft met several times

The interior of the Morgan Library and Museum in New York City

with Morgan and turned to the House of Morgan for loans to finance U.S. affairs overseas. Yet Taft disliked the power of the trusts. During Taft's presidency, the government accused U.S. Steel and another Morgan trust of breaking antitrust laws. Members of Congress attacked what they called the money trust, a term that referred to U.S. bankers who seemed to control so much of the country. To some Americans, Morgan alone was the money trust.

*Arsène Pujo
(1861–1939),
member of the
U.S. Congress
and chair of the
Pujo Committee*

In 1912, Congress investigated the money trust. Morgan was ordered to testify in front of a special committee led by Representative Arsène Pujo. The committee, which came to be called the Pujo Committee, wanted to find out more about the money trust and its power in America.

The lawyer for the committee, Samuel Untermyer, wanted to prove that some banking firms were so powerful that other banks couldn't compete with them. With their money and power, he claimed, they ruled America's major corporations. Untermyer wanted to question Morgan about how he ran his huge, powerful banking firms.

Morgan arrived by train in Washington, D.C., the day before his hearing. With him was an impressive group that included some of the country's top lawyers, an ambassador, a senator, his business partners, his daughter Louisa, and his son Jack. Expect the worst in the committee room, Jack warned him. The popular outcry against trusts was reaching its peak. Morgan's spirits were low, and he was irritable.

That night he played solitaire and smoked one of his favorite cigars.

The next day, December 19, 1912, Morgan appeared before the Pujo Committee. At times, he was a little slower with his thoughts than he once had been. He reminded Untermyer and the committee that he was getting old and hard of hearing. Finally, Untermyer asked Morgan if he disliked competition. "I like a little competition," Morgan replied. He also admitted that he liked business combinations, although he preferred to call them cooperations. When Untermyer claimed that Morgan had vast power, the banker disagreed. The lawyer questioned Morgan's claims that his business actions were good for the country. "And you are acting on that assumption all the time?" Untermyer asked. Morgan replied, "I always do, sir."

Morgan returned to New York a much happier man. His partners believed he had done a good job in Washington, D.C. The woman who ran Morgan's private library noted

> In 1902, Morgan helped create the International Mercantile Marine Company, a type of trust in the shipbuilding industry. It owned companies like the White Star Line, which built and operated luxury ships that sailed between North America and Europe. One of the ships that it built was the Titanic, which sank on April 15, 1912, during its maiden voyage, killing more than 1,500 people. Morgan was scheduled to sail on that voyage but canceled his reservation to vacation longer in France and travel to Venice.

how a bouncing, singing Morgan came to her. He arrived, "putting both arms around me and kissing me on both cheeks," she recalled.

After the Christmas holidays, Morgan traveled to Egypt. At times, he kept the joyful energy he showed after his testimony. But at other times, his old depressed state crept back. Sometimes he had strange thoughts about suicide or strangers who wanted to harm him. His doctor thought the stress of the Pujo Committee was finally affecting him. Throughout his life, Morgan had complained of ailments that doctors couldn't explain. Now he complained more.

That spring, Morgan traveled to Italy. His mental and physical health still had not improved. On March 31, 1913, just weeks before his 76th birthday, J. Pierpont Morgan died in Rome. Flags on Wall Street flew at half-staff, and letters of sympathy arrived in Italy by the thousands. Morgan's body was brought back to New York City, where a huge memorial service was held for him at St. George's Episcopal Church. Morgan was buried in Hartford, the city of his birth.

Newspapers soon reported the details of his will. He left most of his vast fortune to his son Jack. The total value of his estate was about $80 million—almost $1.5 billion today.

Morgan left a legacy of wealth, power, art, books, and philanthropy. But he left behind much more than

Funeral procession for J. Pierpont Morgan in Hartford, Connecticut

that. Although he was not always pleasant or well-liked, he was trusted by many Americans. He served as a sort of central banker for the country when it didn't have one. He helped banks, businesses, and the government through many difficult financial times.

Nine months after Morgan's death, the United States established the Federal Reserve System, a central banking system that didn't rely on private bankers to keep the nation financially strong. But Morgan had helped the United States avoid economic disaster more than once. As he had hoped, his efforts had made the country stronger. ❧

MORGAN'S LIFE

1857

Starts his business career at Duncan, Sherman & Company in New York City

1854

Graduates from high school

1837

Born in Hartford, Connecticut, April 17

1850

1840

Auguste Rodin, famous sculptor of *The Thinker*, is born

1856

The Treaty of Paris ends the Crimean War, which was fought between Russia and the armies of Britain, France, Sardinia, and the Ottoman Empire (modern-day Turkey)

1858

English scientist Charles Darwin presents his theory of evolution to a gathering of scientists

WORLD EVENTS

1861

Marries Amelia "Memie" Sturges; she dies four months after the wedding, in 1862

1862

Establishes J.P. Morgan & Company

1864

Becomes a partner in Dabney, Morgan & Company

1860

1860

Postage stamps are widely used throughout the world

1862

Victor Hugo publishes *Les Misérables*

1863

Construction begins on the first transcontinental railroad in Sacramento, California

MORGAN'S LIFE

1865

Marries Frances "Fanny" Louise Tracy

1869

Rescues the Albany and Susquehanna Railroad from hostile investors; helps found the American Museum of Natural History

1871

Becomes a partner in Drexel, Morgan & Company

1870

1865

Lewis Carroll writes *Alice's Adventures in Wonderland*

1869

The periodic table of elements is invented by Dimitri Mendeleyev

WORLD EVENTS

1882

Installs electric
lights in his home
and office

1885

Settles a battle
between New
York Central and
Pennsylvania
railroads

1873

Helps some U.S.
banks survive the
Panic of 1873

1880

1886

Grover Cleveland
dedicates the
Statue of Liberty
in New York, a gift
from the people
of France

1873

Ivy League schools
draw up the first
rules for American
football

1881

Booker T.
Washington
founds Tuskegee
Institute

MORGAN'S LIFE

1890

Becomes the
head of the
House of Morgan

1895

Arranges deal
to end the U.S.
government's
shortage of gold

1901

Creates U.S.
Steel, the
world's first
billion-dollar
company

1900

1893

Women gain
voting privileges
in New Zealand,
the first country
to take such
a step

1896

The first modern
Olympic Games
are held in
Athens, Greece

1901

Britain's Queen
Victoria dies

WORLD EVENTS

1912

Appears before the
Pujo Committee

1913

Dies in
Rome, Italy,
March 31

1907

Arranges loans
that soften the
damage of the
Panic of 1907

1910

1913

Henry Ford
begins to
use standard
assembly lines
to produce
automobiles

1909

The National
Association for
the Advancement
of Colored People
(NAACP) is founded

DATE OF BIRTH: April 17, 1837

BIRTHPLACE: Hartford, Connecticut

FATHER: Junius Spencer Morgan (1813–1890)

MOTHER: Juliet Pierpont Morgan (1816–1884)

FIRST SPOUSE: Amelia "Memie" Sturges (1835–1862)

DATE OF MARRIAGE: 1861

SECOND SPOUSE: Frances "Fanny" Louise Tracy (1842–1924)

DATE OF MARRIAGE: May 3, 1865

CHILDREN: Louisa Pierpont Morgan Satterlee (1866–1946)
John "Jack" Pierpont Morgan Jr. (1867–1943)
Juliet Morgan (1870–1952)
Anne Morgan (1873–1952)

DATE OF DEATH: March 31, 1913

PLACE OF BURIAL: Hartford, Connecticut

FURTHER READING

Byman, Jeremy. *J.P. Morgan: Banker to a Growing Nation*. Greensboro, N.C.: Morgan Reynolds, 2001.

Condon, Daniel. *Playing the Market: Stocks and Bonds*. Chicago: Heinemann Library, 2003.

Halpern, Monica. *Railroad Fever: Building the Transcontinental Railroad, 1830–1870*. Washington, D.C.: National Geographic, 2004.

Stefoff, Rebecca. *Growth in America: 1865–1914*. New York: Benchmark Books, 2003.

LOOK FOR MORE SIGNATURE LIVES BOOKS ABOUT THIS ERA:

Amelia Earhart: *Legendary Aviator*
ISBN 0-7565-1880-6

Thomas Alva Edison: *Great American Inventor*
ISBN 0-7565-1884-9

Langston Hughes: *The Voice of Harlem*
ISBN 0-7565-0993-9

Wilma Mankiller: *Chief of the Cherokee Nation*
ISBN 0-7565-1600-5

Eleanor Roosevelt: *First Lady of the World*
ISBN 0-7565-0992-0

Franklin Delano Roosevelt: *The New Deal President*
ISBN 0-7565-1586-6

Elizabeth Cady Stanton: *Social Reformer*
ISBN 0-7565-0990-4

Gloria Steinem: *Champion of Women's Rights*
ISBN 0-7565-1587-4

Amy Tan: *Writer and Storyteller*
ISBN 0-7565-1876-8

Booker T. Washington: *Innovative Educator*
ISBN 0-7565-1881-4

On the Web

For more information on *J. Pierpont Morgan,* use FactHound.

1. Go to *www.facthound.com*
2. Type in this book ID: 0756518903
3. Click on the *Fetch It* button.

FactHound will find the best Web sites for you.

Historic Sites

The Museum of American Finance
48 Wall St.
New York, NY 10004
212/908-4110
Displays historical facts and items about Wall Street and the stock market

The Morgan Library
29 E. 36th St.
New York, NY 10016
212/590-0300
A collection of art, artifacts, and books owned by J. Pierpont Morgan

bonds
papers that show a person has loaned money to a company or government and will receive a larger amount in return

brokers
people who buy and sell stocks and bonds

industrialists
people who own large factories

investors
people who put money into a company so they can share in the profits

mergers
the joining together of two or more companies

philanthropist
a generous donor

plutocrat
someone who influences government by wealth

shares
the small parts into which a company's stock is divided

speculation
buying something not to use but to sell for a higher price later

stock
the value of a company, divided into shares when sold to investors

Wall Street
a narrow street in New York City and the first permanent home of the New York Stock Exchange; also refers to American financial institutions as a whole

Source Notes

Chapter 1

Page 9, line 10: "John Pierpont Morgan and the American Corporation." 25 April 2006. www.gprep.org/fac/sjochs/jpmorgan-1.htm

Page 10, line 6: Jean Strouse. *Morgan: American Financier*. New York: Perennial, 1999, p. 15.

Page 11, line 8: Peter Krass. *Carnegie*. New York: John Wiley & Sons, 2002, p. 409.

Page 12, line 7: *Morgan: American Financier*, p. 403.

Page 13, line 13: Ibid., p. x.

Chapter 2

Page 17, line 23: Ibid., p. 32.

Page 19, line 1: Ibid., p. 35.

Page 19, line 13: Vincent P. Carosso and Rose C. Carosso. *The Morgans: Private International Bankers 1854–1913*. Cambridge, Mass.: Harvard University Press, 1987, p. 27.

Chapter 3

Page 24, line 3: *Morgan: American Financier*, p. 55.

Page 24, line 10: Ibid., p. 65.

Page 26, line 8: *The Morgans: Private International Bankers 1854–1913*, p. 84.

Page 27, line 2: *Morgan: American Financier*, p. 73.

Page 31, line 7: Ibid., p. 91.

Chapter 4

Page 34, line 1: *The Morgans: Private International Bankers 1854–1913*, p. 94.

Page 36, line 4: *Morgan: American Financier*, pp. 111–112.

Page 40, line 4: Edward J. Renehan Jr. *Dark Genius of Wall Street: The Misunderstood Life of Jay Gould, King of the Robber Barons*. New York: Basic Books, 2005, p. 20.

Page 41, line 14: *Morgan: American Financier*, p. 137.

Chapter 5

Page 48, line 3: *The Morgans: Private International Bankers 1854–1913*, p. 181.

Page 49, line 6: Ron Chernow. *The House of Morgan: An American Banking Dynasty and the Rise of Modern Finance*. New York: Atlantic Monthly Press, 1990, p. 37.

Page 50, line 24: *Morgan: American Financier*, p. 211.

Chapter 6

Page 54, line 8: *The Morgans: Private International Bankers 1854–1913*, p. 270.

Page 54, line 25: Stanley Jackson. *J.P. Morgan: A Biography*. New York: Stein and Day, 1983, p. 129.

Page 56, line 14: *Morgan: American Financier*, p. 206.

Page 57, line 26: Ibid., p. 548.

Chapter 7

Page 61, line 6: *The Morgans: Private International Bankers 1854–1913*, p. 233.

Page 61, sidebar: Brian Trumbore. "Homestake Gold Mine Part 3." 27 April 2006. www.buyandhold.com/bh/en/education/history/2001/homestake3.html

Page 63, line 10: *The House of Morgan: An American Banking Dynasty and the Rise of Modern Finance*, p. 55.

Page 65, line 9: *Morgan: American Financier*, p. 280.

Chapter 8

Page 70, line 22: John Morton Blum. *The National Experience: A History of the United States*. 4th ed. New York: Harcourt Brace Jovanovich, 1977, p. 482.

Page 72, line 26: *Morgan: American Financier*, p. 341.

Page 74, line 15: Ibid., p. 345.

Page 75, line 1: Ibid., p. 351.

Chapter 9

Page 81, line 4: Ibid., p. 375.

Page 81, line 14: *The House of Morgan: An American Banking Dynasty and the Rise of Modern Finance*, p. 99.

Page 82, line 3: Ibid., p. 92.

Page 83, line 8: Edmund Morris. *Theodore Rex*. New York: Random House, 2001, p. 92.

Page 83, line 20: *Annals of America*, Volume 12. Chicago: Encyclopaedia Britannica, 1968, p. 579.

Page 84, line 23: *The Morgans: Private International Bankers 1854–1913*, p. 456.

Chapter 10

Page 88, line 7: Ibid., p. 540.

Page 88, line 9: *The House of Morgan: An American Banking Dynasty and the Rise of Modern Finance*, p. 122.

Page 88, line 28: Ibid., p. 536.

Page 89, line 9: *Morgan: American Financier*, p. 579.

Page 90, sidebar: *The House of Morgan: An American Banking Dynasty and the Rise of Modern Finance*, p. 128.

Page 93, line 10: *Morgan: American Financier*, p. 10.

Page 93, line 20: Ibid., p. 12.

Page 94, line 2: Ibid., p. 671.

Select Bibliography

Annals of America, Volumes 12 and 13. Chicago: Encyclopaedia Britannica, 1968.

Blum, John Morton. *The National Experience: A History of the United States*. 4th ed. New York: Harcourt Brace Jovanovich, 1977.

Carosso, Vincent P., and Rose C. Carosso. *The Morgans: Private International Bankers 1854–1913*. Cambridge, Mass.: Harvard University Press, 1987.

Chernow, Ron. *The House of Morgan: An American Banking Dynasty and the Rise of Modern Finance*. New York: Atlantic Monthly Press, 1990.

Foner, Eric, and John Arthur Garraty. *The Reader's Companion to American History*. Boston: Houghton Mifflin, 1990.

Jackson, Stanley. *J.P. Morgan: A Biography*. New York: Stein and Day, 1983.

Josephson, Matthew. *Edison: A Biography*. New York: John Wiley, 1992.

Krass, Peter. *Carnegie*. New York: John Wiley & Sons, 2002.

Morris, Edmund. *Theodore Rex*. New York: Random House, 2001.

Olson, James Stuart. *Encyclopedia of the Industrial Revolution in America*. Westport, Conn.: Greenwood Press, 2002.

Pierpont Morgan Library. *In August Company: The Collections of the Pierpont Morgan Library*. New York: Pierpont Morgan Library, 1993.

Renehan, Edward J., Jr. *Dark Genius of Wall Street: The Misunderstood Life of Jay Gould, King of the Robber Barons*. New York: Basic Books, 2005.

Strouse, Jean. *Morgan: American Financier*. New York: Perennial, 1999.

Michael Burgan is a freelance writer of books for children and adults. A history graduate of the University of Connecticut, he has written more than 90 fiction and nonfiction children's books. For adult audiences, he has written news articles, essays, and plays. Michael Burgan is a recipient of an Educational Press Association of America award.

Image Credits